Putting the Pieces Together

Seeking Answers to Life's

Most Important Questions

Richard B. Ramsay

Putting the Pieces Together

Seeking Answers to Life's Most Important Questions

Richard B. Ramsay

ISBN: 979-8-90148-570-5

Staten House

"Is there still an up and a down?"

"Aren't we straying as though through an infinite nothing?"

Nietzsche's "madman" shouts these questions as he runs around the marketplace, facing the consequences of not believing in God.

"Nobody expects when he gets aboard a train to be taken where he wants to go."

The "switchman" in the short story by Juan José Arreola tells the traveler that if he is lucky enough to catch a train, it may not take him to his desired destination. Some people ride around for years and finally decide to get off the train in some remote location, and others just stay on board until they die.

"What? Where from? Where to?"

The famous artist Gaugin painted a picture with this title. At one side you see a baby, and when you follow across to the other side, you see the figure of an old woman who is dying.

How about you?

-Do you sometimes wonder where we came from and where we are going? What's the destination of the train we're on?

-Do you ask yourself if God exists and if there is life after death?

-Why are we here? Are we just flying through "an infinite nothing"?

-How do you know what is right and what is wrong? Is there an "up" and a "down"?

-Wouldn't you like to know why there is so much suffering and evil and how it can be fixed?

-How about truth itself? How can you be sure of anything?

Sometimes life seems like a complicated jigsaw puzzle. This booklet is meant to help you put the pieces together, to seek answers to life's most important questions. As with any puzzle, all pieces must fit together to form a complete picture.

CONTENTS

1. How did we get here? Does God really exist?

There are two main options to explain the existence of the amazing world we live in and the unique characteristics of human beings: either it's the result of an impersonal process such as evolution or it's the work of a personal intelligent designer, a Creator.[i]

Some people, such as the famous physicist Stephen Hawking, argue that we don't need to believe in God to explain the universe. However, if we accept this option as a piece of the puzzle, we will have trouble fitting it in.

First, the details of nature and the characteristics of human beings are difficult to explain simply as a result of an impersonal process. Consider the complex parts and functions of the human body, the delicate beauty of a flower, the changing colors of a sunset, the majesty of the mountains, the vast oceans, and the countless stars. The structure of atoms and the physical laws of the universe are precisely tuned to function properly and to allow the planets to remain in their orbits. If gravity were slightly stronger, the universe would collapse.

Think of the extraordinary inner nature of human beings. How can you explain emotions, logic, creativity, a sense of right and wrong, the gift of enjoying beauty, and the ability to make decisions? The Bible teaches that human beings have been created "in God's image," that is, with some qualities similar to God Himself (see Genesis 1:27).

How about the beginning of everything? The universe could not come to exist out of nothing.

Second, if we ourselves were the product of an impersonal process, we couldn't trust our own convictions. It would mean, as Cabanis said, "The brain secretes thoughts in the same way that the liver secretes bile."[ii] C.S. Lewis argues that our personal convictions would mean no more than the color of our hair.[iii]

This leads inevitably to a self-contradiction. As one scientist recognized, "If my mental processes are determined wholly by the motions of atoms in my brain, I have no reason to suppose that my beliefs are true . . . and hence I have no reason for supposing my brain to be composed of atoms."[iv]

Darwin himself admitted the following in a letter:

> The horrendous doubt always arises whether the convictions of man's mind, which has developed from the mind of the lower animals, are of any value or at all trustworthy. Would anyone trust the convictions of a monkey's mind, if there are any convictions in such a mind?[v]

But we don't really have to prove that God exists. The Bible tells us that people already have an instinctive knowledge in their hearts of His existence and that all of nature speaks of Him (see Romans 1:19-20).

Sometimes we doubt it or we deny it, but God reminds each of us of His presence in the unique way we need it. For C.S. Lewis, it was his sense of joy that made him realize God existed. Joy could not come from an impersonal universe.[vi]

God made me aware that He was real while I was looking at the countless stars one night. Suddenly I sensed His presence and His glory! I realized I knew He was there! I went home that night with a profound new joy in my heart!

2. Why am I here?
What is my purpose?

Again, there are two main categories when considering the purpose of your life: live for yourself or live for someone else.

Nietzsche argued that we should free ourselves from traditional external ethical norms and create our own values. We should avoid "weakness" and strive to be "strong," learning to impose our own will on others.[vii]

If there is no God, the option of living just for yourself, according to your own norms, might be tempting. Why not? However, it leads to ugly consequences, such as broken relationships, cruelty, and injustice.

Some people defend the first option as a natural tendency. Marquis de Sade was known for his perverted lifestyle and for taking pleasure in sexual cruelty, from which the term "sadism" is derived. He wrote:

> By Nature created, created with very keen tastes, with very strong passions; placed on this earth for the sole purpose of yielding to them and satisfying them....[viii]

But most people would admit they have an instinctive sense that selfishness is wrong. The notion is undeniable.

Our sense of right and wrong comes from God Himself, who has made us in His image. The Bible explains that God has engraved some aspects of His moral principles on our hearts.

Since the Fall, we will disagree on many ethical decisions, but at least we all still have a conscience (Romans 2:14-15) and many of us will agree on certain basic concepts.

Jesus summarizes the purpose of life in two main commandments: Love God and love others as yourself. It doesn't mean you should stop caring about yourself. In fact, it's hard to love others if you don't love yourself. But we shouldn't put ourselves first at the expense of others. Think of the "golden rule": Do unto others as you would have them do to you.

The whole Bible gives us ethical guidelines. From the beginning, people were supposed to develop a harmonious society and take care of the creation (Genesis 1 and 2). The Ten Commandments contain principles that most people consider important, such as not lying, stealing or killing. The apostle Paul reminds us that we should do everything to honor God (1 Corinthians 10:31).

The first two pieces of the puzzle fit together perfectly. Since God created us, He should be the center of our lives, and since He made us in His image with a sense of right and wrong, we know instinctively that we should love other people. When we follow these principles, there is harmony. When we don't, it leads to conflict and destruction.

When I was doubting the existence of God, I couldn't see any purpose in my life. In fact, I wondered why I should be good instead of bad. I saw my life like a disorderly page of scribbled notes. But when I realized I knew He was really there, the notes became neat and orderly, with God at the top.

1. Love God.
2. Love others as yourself.

3. What went wrong?
Why is there so much evil and suffering?

The world is beautiful, and we can enjoy so much of life, but there are also terrible problems such as hatred and violence, natural disasters, poverty and hunger, crime and injustice, loneliness and depression. ...What happened?

Could it be the result of an evolutionary process guided by the principle of the survival of the fittest? If so, there really is no right and wrong, just weak and strong. "Might makes right." Or as Marquis de Sade argued, "what *is*, is right."[ix]

An explanation that fits our puzzle better is that God created a good world, then humans broke it. Right and wrong are valid concepts and the world needs to be fixed.

G. K. Chesterton offers the illustration of a person who wakes up with amnesia on the beach of an abandoned island. He finds remnants from another place—jewelry, books, photographs, coins, and fine clothes. He concludes that there has been a shipwreck.[x] This is mankind's situation. We live in a wrecked world, and the Bible explains how it happened.

God made all things beautiful and in harmony (Genesis 1). He created us with a conscience and with the purpose of loving Him and loving each other.

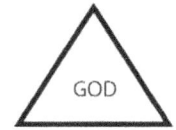

However, the first people (Adam and Eve) made a tragic decision. They turned away from God and disobeyed Him. God had warned them that the result of rejecting Him would be catastrophic. Nevertheless, they chose to live for themselves instead of living according to their intended purpose.

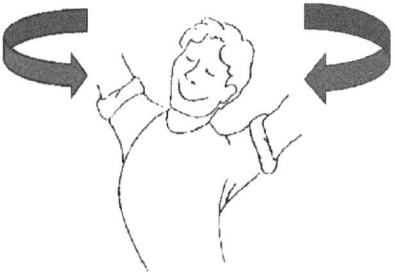

That's what went wrong. That is why there is so much evil and suffering. And the same self-centered disposition continues to plague us (Romans 5:12). The Bible teaches that we are all sinners deserving condemnation (Romans 3).

This has produced conflict between people and God, between people and each other, between people and nature, and even internal conflict within peoples' own hearts.

Often people ask why God would allow this to happen. We can't pretend to understand this fully, but we can assume that God wanted people to be free. He made us in His own image, and that includes the ability to make decisions. God wanted us to love Him and follow Him sincerely, not because we were programmed to do it.

Also, as we will see in the next chapter, God has been solving the problem in a marvelous way ever since things went bad. He is holy and can't simply overlook sin, but He takes the punishment for sin upon Himself in the person of Jesus.

4. How can things be fixed?
Is there hope?

It's easy to become discouraged. Philosopher Albert Camus once said,

> Something is dreadfully wrong. I am a disillusioned and exhausted man. I have lost faith, lost hope, ever since the rise of Hitler. Is it any wonder that, at my age, I am looking for something to believe in?[xi]

There have been many attempts to make the world a better place. Some have built empires or started movements, others have created new philosophies or religions, and still others seek solutions in politics, better laws, science, or medicine. Some of these efforts may help, but they all eventually disappoint us, because they don't really change *people*.

We are broken and we can't fix ourselves. Nature is damaged and it can't heal itself. The conflicts remain. What we need is a *miracle*.

This is the beauty of the Christian message. There *is* something to believe in! Or to be more precise, there is *some-one* to believe in! Jesus, being divine, crossed the cosmic barriers to become also human. He not only showed us how we should live, but He also went to the cross on our behalf. As He suffered the punishment we deserve, Jesus absorbed into Himself sin and evil, like a "black hole" with

19

overwhelming gravity, pulling everything corrupt into the center of His heart.

With His sacrifice and His victorious resurrection, He began the process of restoration (Romans 8:1-4). His Spirit changes our hearts, and as we believe in Jesus, we begin to experience healing in all broken relationships (Colossians 1:19-29).

This process will one day be complete for all eternity. No other religion or philosophy comes even close to promising anything so wonderful!

I remember the first time I really understood what Jesus did for me. I had told a lie and was feeling bad about it. Then I heard a teacher explaining that Jesus died on the cross to forgive our sins, giving examples like stealing or *telling a lie*! I felt like God was speaking to me through her. It was no longer just a biblical doctrine; it was personal!

I once saw an emotional video that illustrates what Jesus has done for us. A man is standing in a forest, surrounded by people who are all handing him objects from the bags they were carrying. He fills his own huge sack with their items until it's almost too heavy to carry. He drags it slowly toward a river, then steps farther and farther into the deep waters pulling the sack with him, until he finally disappears under the surface. The dramatic music continues to play as I wait and wait..., until I finally realize that he has drowned, taking the burdens of everyone else with him. Then suddenly he jumps up out of the water near the other side, without the sack! The music becomes majestic! He is alive again, victorious! What a wonderful way to explain the message of salvation!

How about you? Is there something you feel guilty about? Take it out of your bag and give it to Jesus. Ask Him to forgive you. Then think of Him going to the cross, dying for you, and rising victoriously! He promises to forgive *all* our sins (1 John 1:9). He takes care of it!

5. What happens after I die? Is there life after death?

The two possibilities are obvious: either you stop existing, or you continue somewhere in another form. Which will it be?

When you see the lifeless body of someone you love, you realize that, in a sense, the person is no longer there. You know he or she was always more than just a body. The most important aspect is what we can't see: a soul with a personality. It's mysterious, but you sense that the person continues to exist in another dimension.

The Bible teaches that, when we cross over into the other world, we either go to be in God's presence eternally or we will be separated from Him eternally.

Contrary to what some people think, the Bible doesn't teach that we will be like angels floating around the clouds in the sky playing harps eternally. Rather, God will make a new earth and give us renewed bodies to live there (Romans 8:22-23). The Bible begins with the story of creation, followed by the Fall and corruption (Genesis 1-3), and ends with prophecies of a new creation where everything is restored and improved (Revelation 21-22).

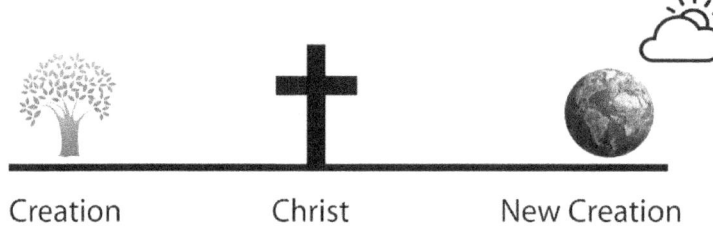

Creation   Christ   New Creation

Think of the most beautiful place you have ever seen in this world and the most wonderful moments you have ever spent with people you love, then multiply it by thousands; we can't even imagine how awesome it will be!

> The Lord is my shepherd; I shall not want. He makes me lie down in green pastures. He leads me beside still waters. ...Even though I walk through the valley of the shadow of death, I will fear no evil, for you are with me; ...and I shall dwell in the house of the LORD forever. (Psalm 23)

Whether you enjoy living in God's presence or not depends on one thing: whether you trust Jesus (John 3:16). You need to decide whether you will ask His forgiveness and follow Him or whether you will reject Him and go your own way.

C.S. Lewis says,

> There are only two kinds of people in the end: those who say to God, "Thy will be done," and those to whom God says, in the end, "Thy will be done."[xii]

Which kind of person will you be?

6. How can I be sure of anything?
If the truth exists, how can I know it?

One final question: How do you know this is true? In fact, how do you know *anything* for sure?

Again, there are two main options: you decide for yourself, or you obtain truth from an authority outside yourself.

The history of philosophy demonstrates that, if you decide for yourself, you can't really be sure of anything. I have experienced that frightening uncertainty for myself.

Some think you can find the truth by observing things and processing them. The problem is that there are an infinite number of things to analyze and everything constantly changes. This inevitably leads to uncertainty.

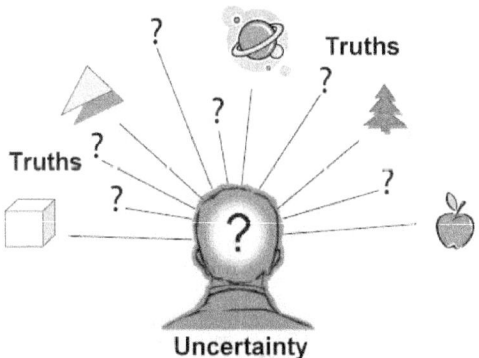

Uncertainty

Another method is to simply use your own reason within your own mind to discern the truth. The problem is that you can't always be sure your reasoning process is functioning accurately. In fact, there are important things beyond a precise grasp of logic such as love and the concept of infinity. Furthermore, you know there is a reality outside your mind that you can't control. If you are standing on the railroad tracks and you see a train coming, you can't simply decide that the train will stop. You have to admit that your own mind isn't the source of truth.

Others might decide that we can't know *anything* for sure. However, you can't live this way. You have to make decisions based on what you believe to be true.

The only way to be sure of knowing the truth is to let God tell you what the truth is. He created everything, knows everything, and graciously reveals the truth to us. Jesus promised that the Holy Spirit would guide us to the truth (John 16:13).

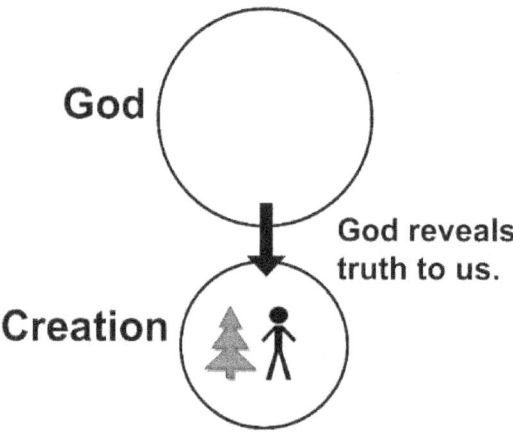

God

God reveals
truth to us.

Creation

God reveals Himself in nature, but His special verbal revelation is found in the Bible. It explains the answers to all the important questions in a coherent package. It tells us how we got here, why we are here, what went wrong, and how to fix it.

If we reject His teachings, we can't fit the pieces together. In fact, the act of rejecting God's truth was the first step in producing conflict and destroying all relationships. Now the first step in restoring things is to believe Him. Jesus said if we follow His Word, we will know the truth and the truth will set us free (John 8.31-32).

I suffered a period of doubt about the Bible. During that time, I was trying to build my own system of truth, one block at a time. However, I realized I couldn't be sure of anything. At the same time, I saw that others like Francis Schaeffer who believed in the Bible enjoyed the certainty of a complete system of truth, giving them insight into all aspects of life: science, history, ethics, languages, philosophy, politics, economics, the arts, ... everything!

This was very attractive to me, but I didn't accept it until I read about how Adam and Eve went off track by questioning God's statements in the Garden of Eden. Cornelius Van Til argued that they had no right to set themselves up as judges over their Creator. I had to admit that I was doing the same thing! I asked God to forgive me, and I told Him I would submit to His Word.

How about you? How do you decide what is true? Do you trust your own mind and your own ability to determine the truth? Does that leave you uncertain? Are you willing to consider God your source of truth?

If you are not familiar with the Bible, I would encourage you to read it with an open mind, willing to listen for the voice of God in it. You might begin by reading one of the gospels. Or maybe you prefer beginning with the first book, Genesis.

Conclusion

I hope that this brief pamphlet has given you convincing answers to some of the most important questions in life. I also hope that it has shown that these answers fit together as a coherent package, that they enable you to put the pieces of the puzzle together.

However, it is not enough to accept these answers in your mind. You will need to take them to heart and make a decision about your life. Jesus died on the cross so that we could be forgiven, He returned to heaven, and He sent the Holy Spirit to be with us and guide us. Christianity is more than a system of truths or a set of ethical principles; it's a personal relationship with God: Father, Son, and Holy Spirit. Simply ask Jesus to forgive you and turn your life over to Him.

If you do, God promises to give you eternal life (John 3:16), and you can begin developing a relationship with Him now. You will sense His presence with you. You can pray to Him and He will communicate with you in different ways, especially in the Bible, His inspired written Word.

Would you like to experience this new life? It's something very personal between you and God, but you could also talk to some Christian who can help you get started! You may want to do further reading on these questions. I also recommend looking for a church that faithfully teaches the Bible, where you feel at home, and where you find Christian friends. Your life will have new meaning and greater joy!

[i] See the arguments of Francis Schaeffer, *He is There and He is Not Silent* (Carol Stream, Illinois: Tyndale House, 2001).

[ii] Cabanis, quoted in James W. Sire, *The Universe Next Door: A Basic Worldview Catalog* (Downers Grove, IL: InterVarsity Press, 1997), 98.

[iii] C. S. Lewis, *Miracles* (New York: Macmillan, 1968), 108.

[iv] J. B. S. Haldane, *Possible Worlds and Other Essays* (London: Chatto & Windus, 1937), quoted by C. S. Lewis in *Miracles*, 22.

[v] Letter to W. Graham (July 3, 1881), quoted in *The Autobiography of Charles Darwin and Selected Letters* (New York: Dover, 1892, new printing, 1958).

[vi] C. S. Lewis, *Surprised by Joy* (Orlando, FL: Harcourt Brace and Company, 1955).

[vii] "La voluntad de dominio" *Los filósofos modernos* (Madrid: Biblioteca de Autores Cristianos, 1976), 247.

[viii] Marquis de Sade, "Dialogue between a Priest and a Dying Man," Justine, Philosophy in the Bedroom, and Other Writings, trans. Austryn Wainhouse and Richard Seaver (Jackson, TN: Grove Press, 1994), 165–66, 174.

[ix] Schaeffer, *He is There and He is Not Silent*, 26.

[x] G. K. Chesterton, quoted by Philip Yancey in *Soul Survivor* (New York: Doubleday, 2001), 51, 52.

[xi] Howard Mumma, *Albert Camus and the Minister* (Brewster, MA: Paraclete Press, 2000), 13–14.

[xii] *The Great Divorce*, 72.